Echoes and Originals: A Poetic Dialogue Between Human and AI

By Lisa Craddock

Prologue

This collection of poems has been with me for some time, without a clear home in any of my other projects—though, admittedly, I tend to revisit similar themes! When I discovered ChatGPT, I thought I had found the answer to my lingering writing insecurities. The tool has been incredibly helpful for my short stories and larger projects, offering clarity in areas like spelling and grammar.

However, when it came to my poetry, I noticed something curious. The AI's translations of my poems often missed the mark—sometimes subtly, other times significantly. These differences between what I intended and what the AI interpreted were intriguing, so much so that I felt they deserved a closer look.

Poetry, after all, comes from the heart. It's not just about structure or correctness; it's about conveying emotion, nuance, and meaning—something that, in my opinion, only an artist can fully achieve. In this collection, I've included both my original words and ChatGPT's interpretations, hoping to spark an interesting conversation about the intersection of creativity, technology, and human expression.

ChatGPT:

I see you there,
Lingering in the shadow of my circus,
Watching as I pull tricks from thin air.
I wonder,
What makes me believe
This life is what I truly want,
When, in truth,
I long to be more like you—
Observing,
Contemplating,
Studying the fool with the painted-on smile.
I wish to step outside my sitcom
And see my own illusions through your eyes.
I long to understand why I see yearning
In your gaze—
What could be alluring about this fool's paradise?
Would I still see that same longing
If I weren't standing on my head?

It's hard to feel excitement
For someone who's content with my world
Just as it is,
Because I'm certain of the change,
Sure this is just a phase.
Will that longing persist
When this change has passed?
Will you then yearn for the days
When I entertained the masses
By exposing my flaws?
Eventually, I'll run out of flaws to reveal,
Leaving nothing but this mundane self
To entertain you with.
What will your eyes say then?
My guess is,
Those lovely eyes will ask,
"Who else is in this room?"

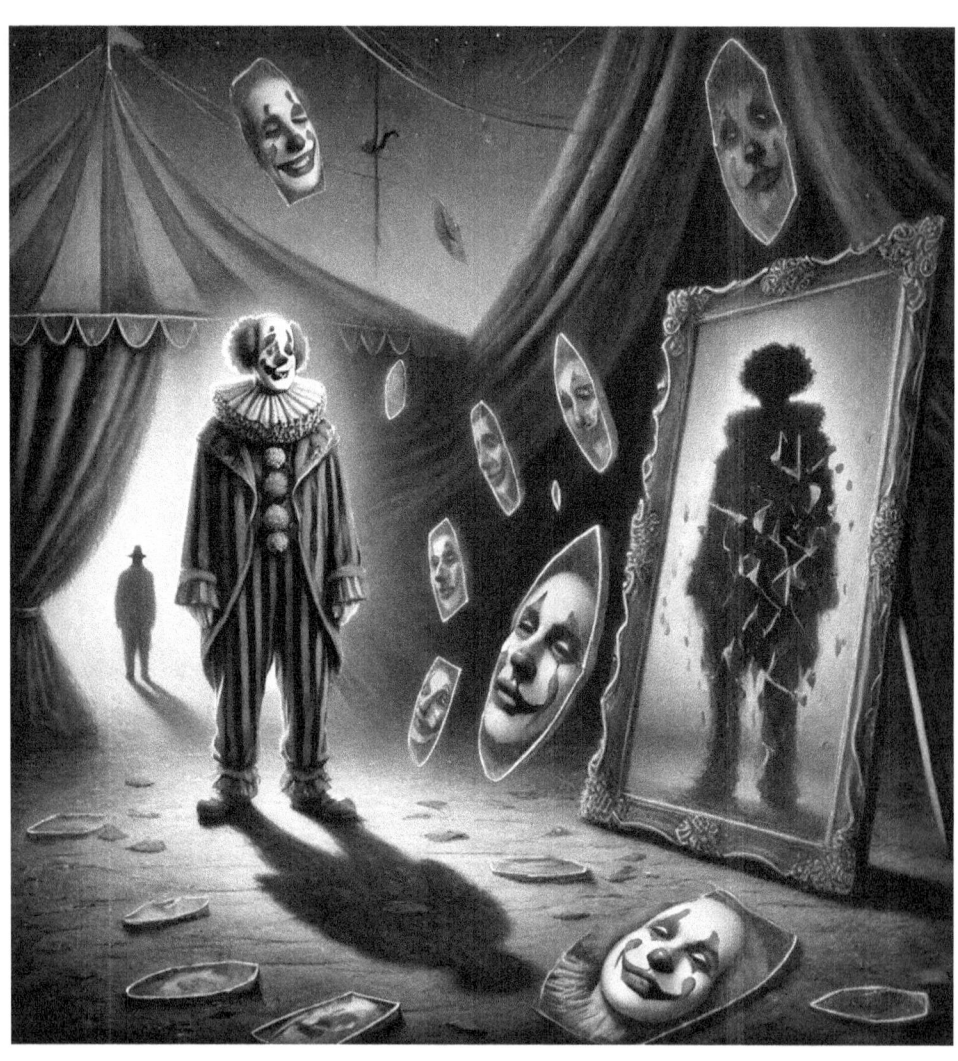

Me:

I see you back there,
Standing In the shadow of my circus,
Watching me pull tricks from my ass,
I'm wondering,
What makes me believe,
This life is what I want,
When in truth
I wish to be more like you
Watching
Wondering,
Speciating the fool with the painted on smile,
I wish to step outside my sitcom,
And see my bullshit threw your eyes,
I wish to know why I see longing in your eyes,
What could possibly be sexy about this fools paradise?
Would I see that same longing,
If I weren't standing on my head?
I find it hard to get excited
For someone who's pleased with my world,
Now, the way it is
Because I'm sure of the change,
I'm sure this is a phase,
And will the longing still be there
When this change has passed?

Will you then long for the days
When I was entertaining the masses
With the exposure of my flaws,
Because eventually,
I will run out of flaws to expose,
And have nothing left but this boring bitch
To entertain you with
What will your eyes say then?
My guess is
Those lovely eyes will say
Who else is in this room?

ChatGPT:

I think she's searching for an escape hatch,
A way out of this body, weary of its limits.
I've heard her voice declare she's had enough,
Witnessed her prayers, pleading to be taken now.
I believe she's willed this plight upon herself—
She's ventured to the edge and returned,
Yet found the journey left her wanting more.
She craves more wrongs than there truly are,
And so, it seems, more wrongs have come to be.

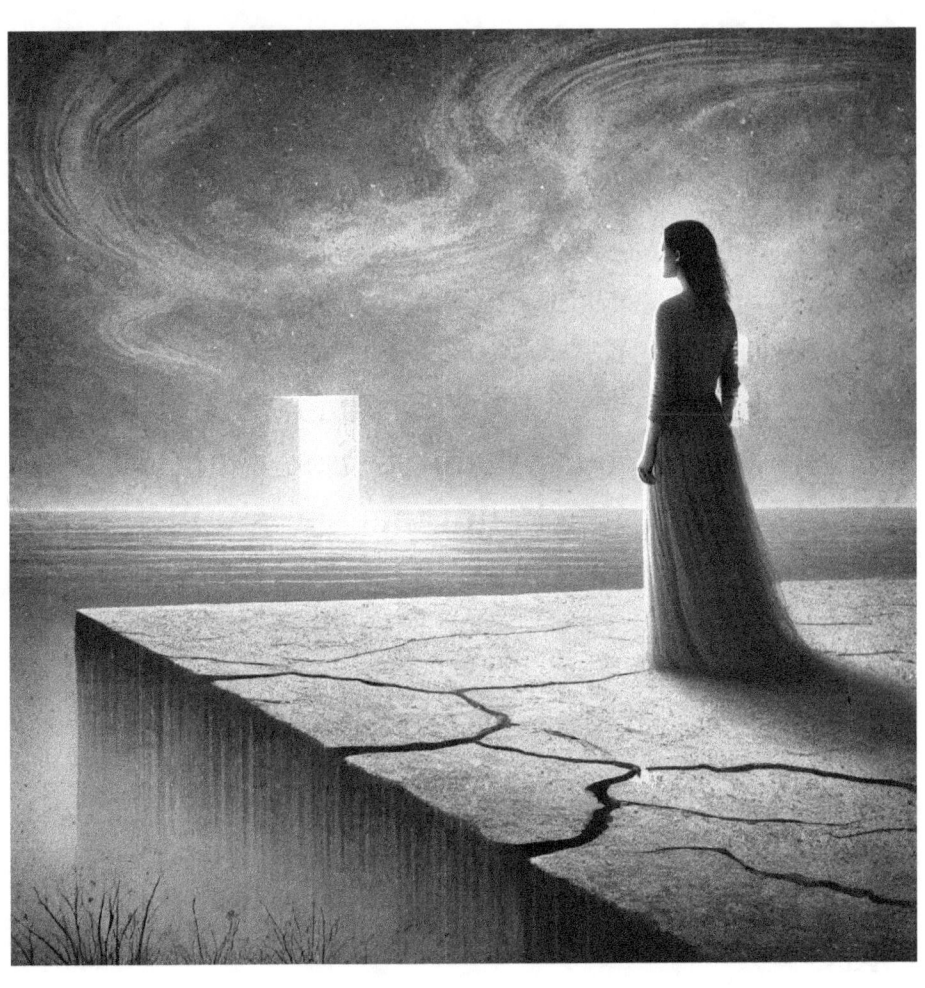

Me:

I think she's looking for an escape hatch,
A way out of that body cause she's sick of it,
I have heard her say she has had enough,
I have witness her prayers to be taken now,
And so I have this belief that she's willed this situation on herself
She has been to the edge and back again,
She has found the whole experience left her wanting,
She wants there to be more wrong with her than there is,
And so now there is more wrong than there was,

ChatGPT:

Poetry is a shadowed realm where I seek to make my mark,
Every line, every phrase meant to stir the soul,
Yet in truth, there's no way to voice the deepest self,
Because the truth is,
I'm lost in uncertainty,
Speculating on what lies beyond,
Pulling words from thin air, as unremarkable as Monday's refuse.
The truth is,
I toy with language,
And to some, that's called art.

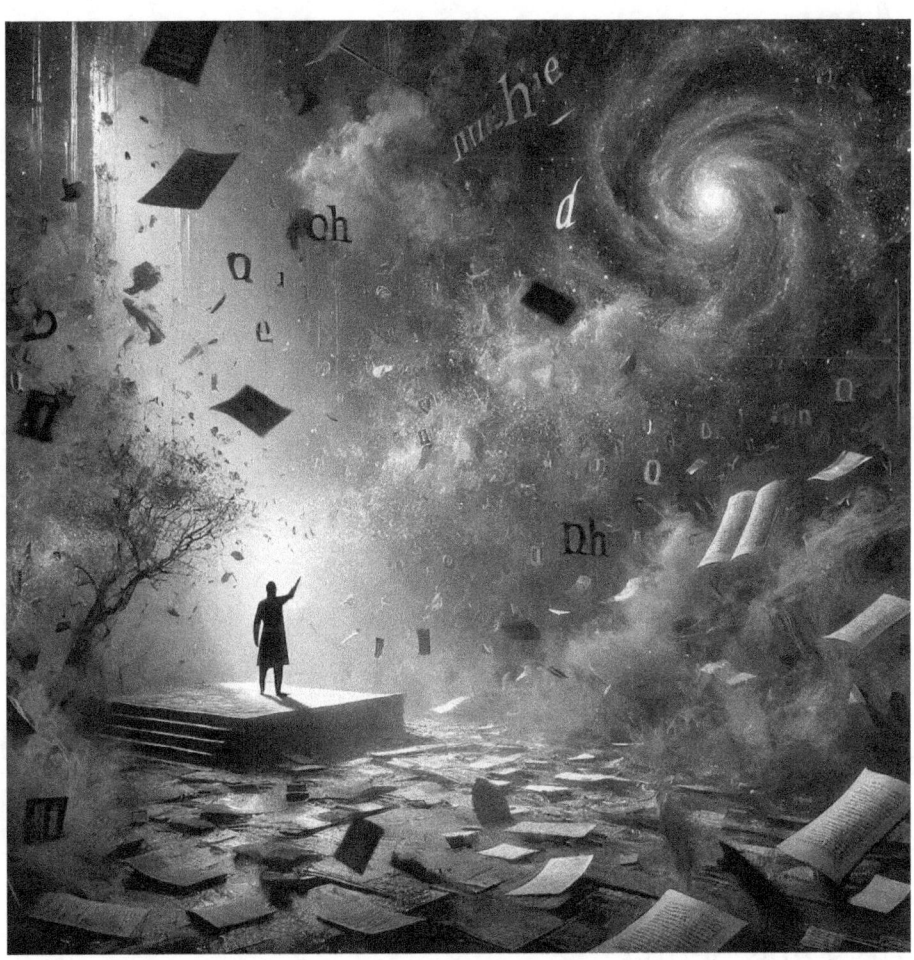

Me:

Poetry is such a dark place to try to make your mark,
every line, every phrase is supposed move its reader
when in reality there is no way to give voice to inner truth,
because the truth is,
I have no idea,
I'm only speculating on there here after,
pulling shit out of my ass as funky as the Monday trash,
the truth is
I play with verbiage
and that's considered art
to some people,

ChatGPT:

When I think of you, my heart feels as if it's shifting from one part of me to another,
Seeking a refuge, almost as if it's trying to hide.
You have the power to inflict pain,
And my body instinctively tries to shield itself.

They say we desire what we cannot have,
I wanted you when I thought you were within reach,
I want you now, even though I know you're not.
Another myth falls away in my book.

I wished to prove that love is worth it,
Yet you are harder to convince than I am,
And my own willingness falters too easily,
Making us both a lost cause.

I let thoughts of you drift in and out of my mind,
Even knowing I don't dwell in yours.
I let jealousy take hold,
Even though I know I have no claim.

If you could choose, you'd be in her arms,
If I could choose, you'd be in mine.
No one's desires are fulfilled here,
And there's something sorrowful in that.

I've decided to move you to the friend zone,
Because I can't imagine life without you.
Even there, you make my heart shift,
You're a danger to my soul from any distance.

I will date again, love again, and move past you,
Yet I'll always wonder if we could have made it,
If there was a place for us.
I'll always believe we could have been great,
Could have had forever,
If I weren't so afraid and you weren't so unwilling.

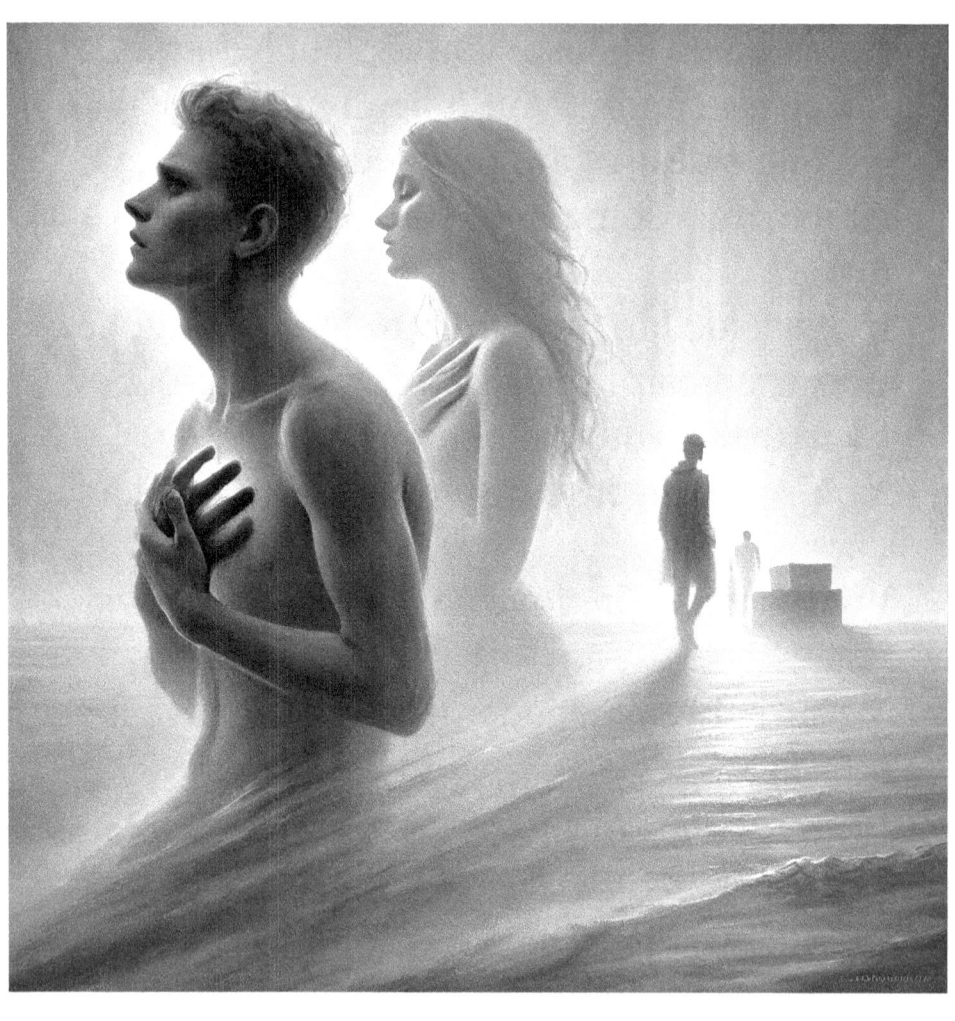

Me:

When I think of you, my heart feels as though it's shifting from one section of my body to the next, almost like it's looking for a place to hide,
You have the power to cause me pain,
My body is trying to protect itself from that,

It has been said that we want what we can't have,
I wanted you when I thought I could have you,
I want you now even though I know I can't,
Another myth bites the dust in my book,

My desire was to prove to us both that love is worth it,
You are harder to convince than I,
And I give up too easy
Which makes us both a lost cause,

I allow your thought to drift in and out of my mind
Even when I know I'm not on yours,
I allow my jealousy to take control,
Even when I know I have no rights,

If you had your choice, you be nestled in her arms,
If I had my choice, you'd be in mine,
Nobody is getting their way here,
There's something sad about that,

I have decided to move you to friend zone,
Because I can't see life without you at all,
Even in the zone you make my heart shift places,
You're dangerous to my soul from anywhere,

I will date again, love again, and move beyond you,
And always I'll wonder if we could have made it,
If there was a place for us,
Always I know we could have been great,
Would could have had forever,
If I weren't so scared and you weren't so unwilling.

ChatGPT:

Because I can't join in the ritual,
I grow to despise it.
Because I don't know the words to the song,
I refuse to dance.

This is what happens when my gaze trails after her,
Because I can't hold onto a girlfriend of my own,
I find myself longing for someone else's.

If luck in love eludes me,
Then surely, it should elude everyone.

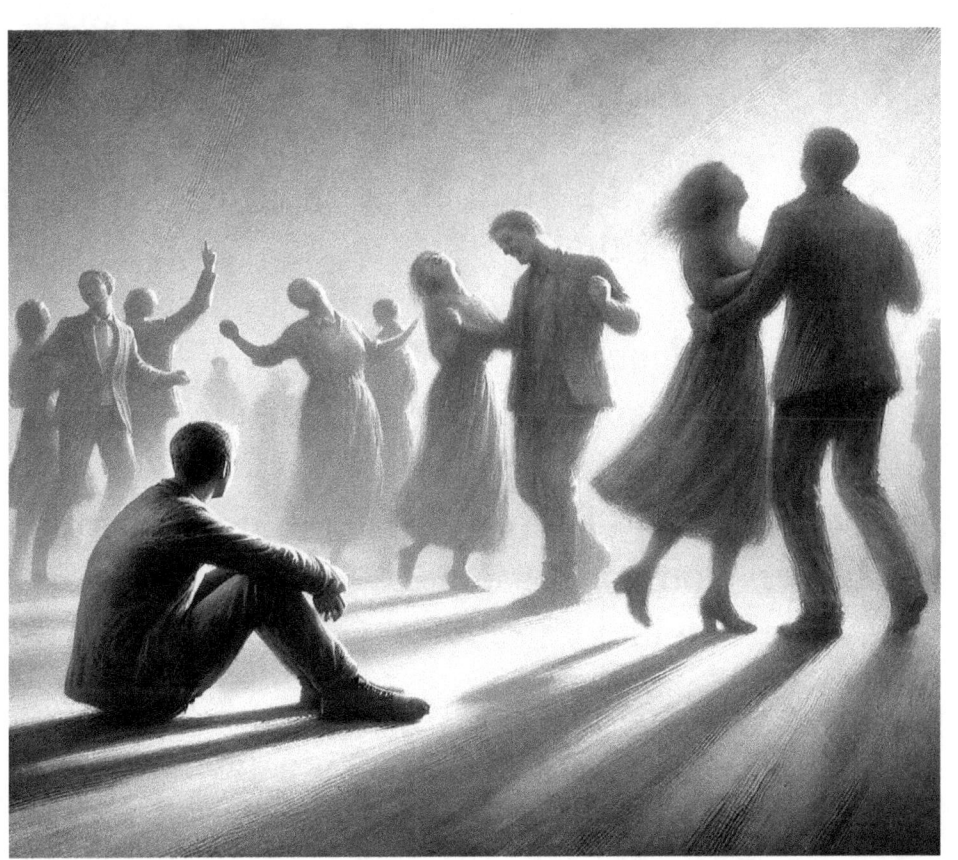

Me:

Because I can't participate in the ritual
I despise the ritual.
Because I don't know the words to the song,
I refuse to dance,
this is what happens when my eyes follow her ass,
Because I can't keep a girlfriend of my own,
I lust for someone else's
If I can't be lucky in love,
No one can.

ChatGPT:

Please grow,
For your own sake,
And for mine.
Don't remain ensnared by this jealousy
That you mistakenly believe is your right,
Just because your parents communicated this way.

Learn that we don't have to be apples
Falling from the same tree.
We are fruit with feet,
Endowed with freedom and the potential to be more—
More than the education we were given,
More than what establishments want us to be.

Develop the ability to accept criticism.
Understand that not every comment about you
Is a personal attack.
Desire more than the simple things
Fed to you by television.

Stop believing that your TV tells the truth.
Realize that your excuses

Are just a sliding glass door
That has been used before.
You are easy to analyze
Because your experiences are naïve.

Deep down, in the folds of your heart,
You may not know what to wish for
Because your guides have let you down,
Leaving your future planning solely up to you.
This is a daunting task
Without the maturity to see through
One's own illusions
And pinpoint one's own truth.

At your age,
Your excuses are thin,
And your voice grows louder
Without making your point clearer.
So for your own sake,
And for the sake of my ink,
And hopefully not a waste of paper,
Open your eyes to growth
And heed what has already been said.

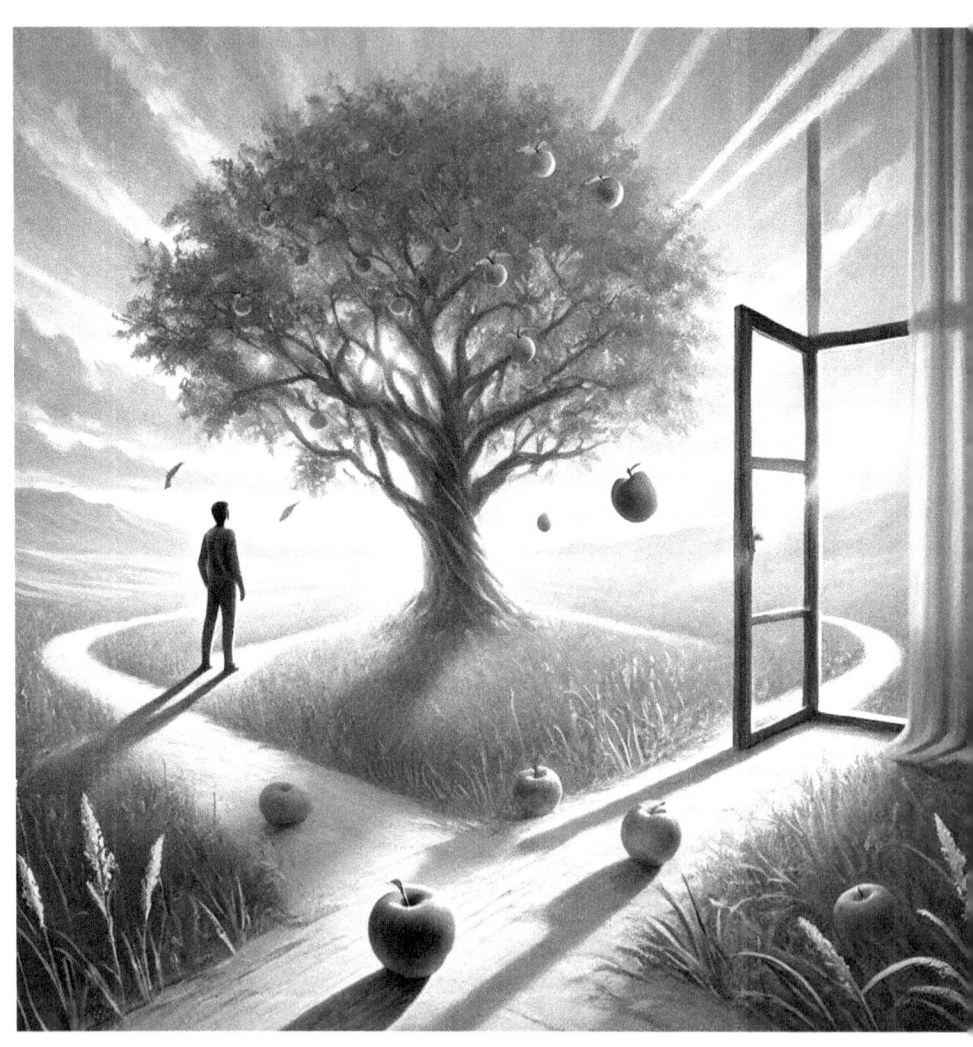

Me:

Please learn,
That we don't have to be apples
To fall from a tree,
We are fruit with feet,
And freedom,
And an ability to be more,
More than the education offered us,
More than the establishment wants us to be,
Please develop an ability to take criticism,
Know that everything said about you,
Is not a direct attack on you,
Please desire more,
Than the simple things you see on tv,
Please stop believing your tv spits the truth,
Please realize that your excuses
Are a plan as a sliding glass door,
And have been told before,
You are as easy to analyze
Because your experience is virginal,
Please believe that deep down,
In the crease of your heart,
You have no idea what to wish for,
Because your tour guides have failed you,
They have left the planning of your future totally up to you,

Which is impossible to do,
Without a mature level to see through
One's own bullshit,
And the ability to put the finger on your truth,
At your age,
Your shit making excuses
And can't stop talking long enough to realize,
So you just get louder,
Your point won't make more sense,
So for your own sake,
And my ink,
And hopefully not a waste of paper,
Open your eyes to growth and see,
What has already been said,

ChatGPT:

I use my pen to breathe,
And my lungs to inspire,
Yet my eyes and ears
Receive little of my attention.

I use my tongue to please,
And my family for balance,
Still, I stumble,
For my heart cannot discern malice.

I use my words to shape,
And my dreams to ignite,
But I remain alone
At the end of each night.

I use my hair for change,
And my heart to allure,
My funds go to habits,
I'll make no excuse.

I'll use this life to learn,
And what I've learned to grow,

Expecting no applause
At the end of my show.

For I've wielded my gifts for sport,
And shone my light on the mean,
Repeating my mistakes,
While killing this dream.

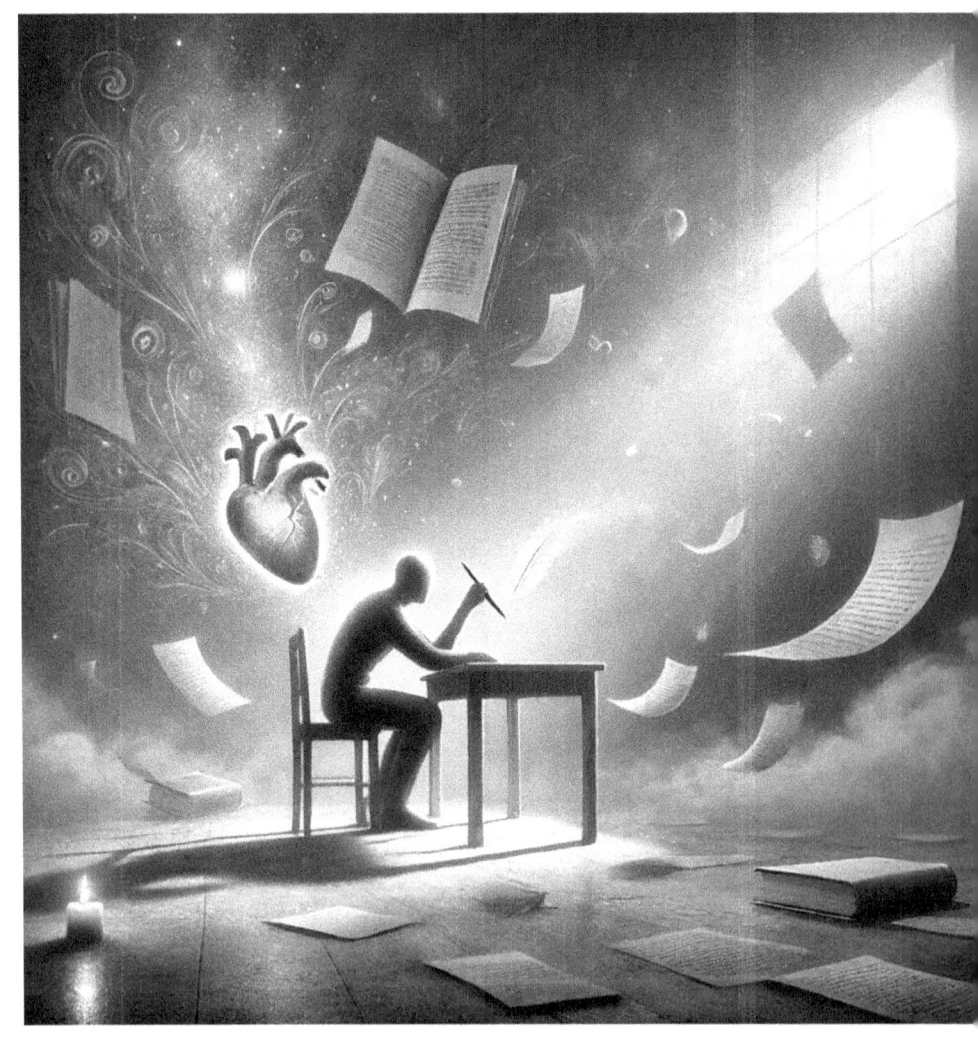

Me:

I use my pen to breath,
and my lungs to induce,
but my eyes and ears,
get very little use,

I use my tongue to please,
and my family for balance,
and still I stumble,
Because my heart can't see malice,

I use my words to mold,
and my dreams to excite,
and still I'm alone
at the end of each night,

I use my hair for change,
and my heart to seduce,
my funds go to addictions,
I'll make no excuse,

I'll use this life to learn,
and what I've learned to grow,
and expect no applause,
At the end of my show,

because I've used my gifts for sport,
and my light on the mean,
repeating my mistakes,
while killing this dream,

ChatGPT:

You are a forbidden desire,
So I shouldn't know the beauty of your eyes,
I shouldn't long for their glance to reach my soul,
I shouldn't recognize the fire burning within them,
But I do.

Someone else holds your hand,
So I shouldn't know its softness,
I shouldn't trace its contours in my mind,
I shouldn't shiver at the thought of those hands,
But I do.

Someone else has claimed your scent,
So I shouldn't know it like my own,
I shouldn't savor it still lingering on my sheets,
I shouldn't discern its taste,
But I do.

Someone else has staked a claim on your heart,
So I shouldn't see the fragility of that claim,
I shouldn't recognize your heart's yearning for freedom,

I shouldn't urge it to stand alone,
But I do.

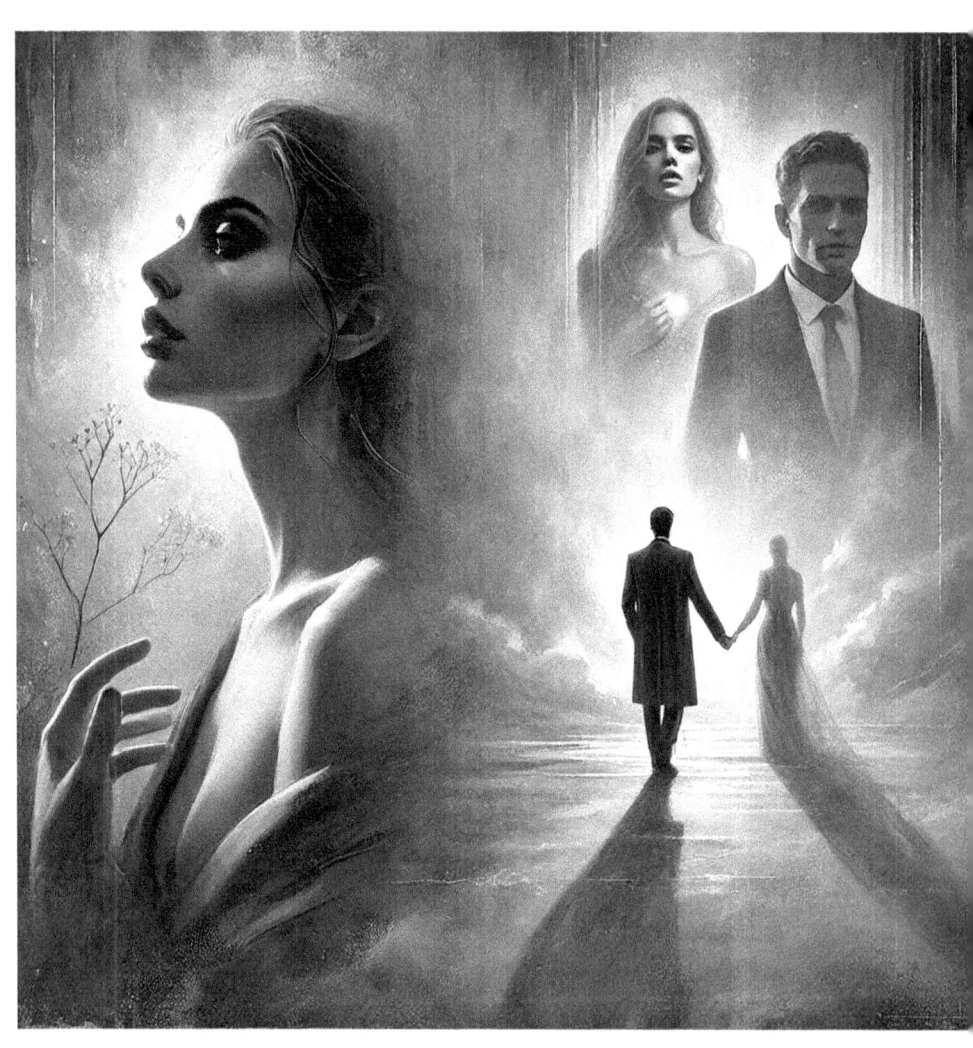

Me:

You are a forbidden wants,
So I shouldn't know how lovely your eyes are,
I shouldn't long for them to peak at my soul,
I shouldn't recognize when the fire is within those eyes,
But I do,

Some one else is holding your hand,
So I shouldn't know how soft those hands are,
I shouldn't be able to sketch a map of its terrain,
I shouldn't arch at the thought of those hands,
But I do,

Some one else has purchased your scent,
So I shouldn't know it like I know my own,
I shouldn't savior it still on my sheets,
I shouldn't know the nature of its taste,
But I do,

Someone else has laid claims on your heart,
So I shouldn't know this claim has false roots,
I shouldn't know this hearts dream of freedom,
I shouldn't encourage this heart to stand alone,
But I do

ChatGPT:

I hate that you don't always return my calls,
I hate that I strive to meet your moods while mine go unmet,
I hate that you don't feel for me the way I feel for you,
I hate this unreturned longing that consumes me,
I hate having to harbor such resentment.

I hate walking on eggshells for women in my life who don't deserve it,
I hate walking on eggshells at all.
I hate that I feel the constant need to care for everyone,
While no one seems willing to care for me.

I hate asking for things from those who couldn't care less,
I hate enduring people's shit for a living.
I hate when others speak of someone and I can't help but see something different,
I hate that you don't think about me—

I hate that you don't think about me,
I hate that you don't think about me,
And I am always,
Always,
Always,
Thinking about you.

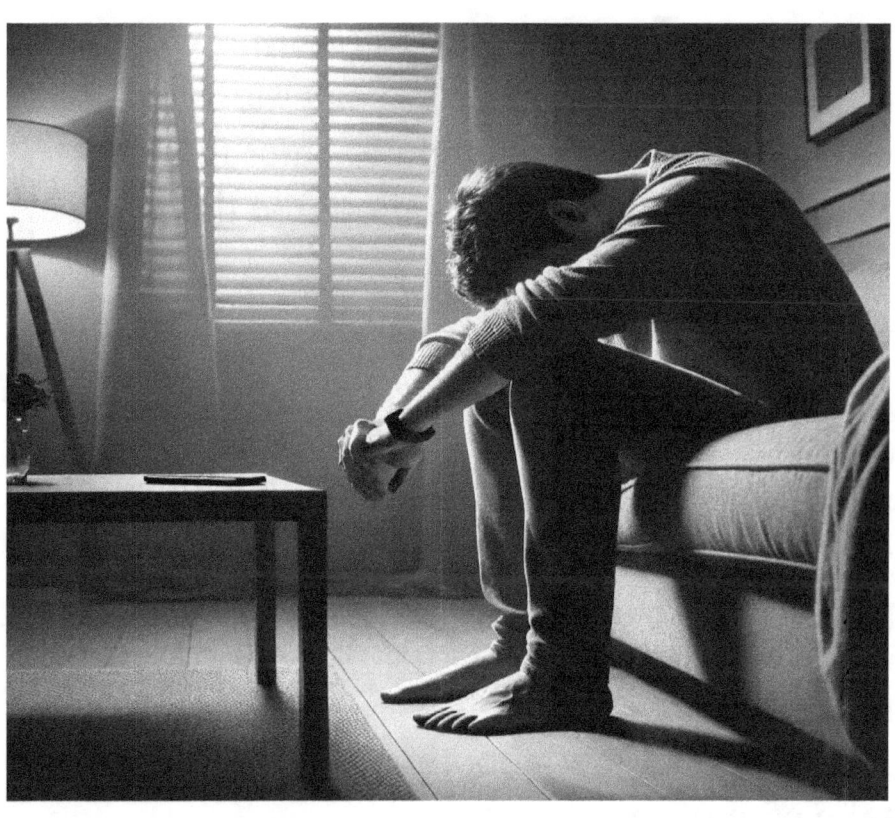

Me:

I hate that you don't always return my calls
I hate that I try very hard to cater to your moods but you never seem to cater to mine
I hate that you don't feel about me the way I feel about you
I hate feeling this way about you when it isn't returned
I hate having to hate things
I hate walking on eggshells for the women in my life when they don't deserve it
I hate walking on eggshells period
I hate the fact that I feel the need to take care of everyone
I hate the fact that nobody seems to WANT to take care of me
I hate asking for shit from people who don't give a shit
I hate taking people shit for a living
I hate when everyone says something about a person and I refuse to believe it because for some crazy reason I think I see something else,
I hate the fact that you don't think about me
I hate the fact that you don't think about me
I hate the fact that you don't think about me
And I am always

Always
Always
Thinking about you!!!

ChatGPT:

Chase me, and I will run;
Flee, and I will pursue.
It's not in our nature for simple touch—
This game we play
To fulfill our social needs.

I've grown weary of this thought,
Tired of my desire to endure you,
Weary of this endless cycle, my dear.
I'm done with the notion
That I must tolerate you.

Sleeping alone means
Never waking because your partner rolled away,
Sleeping alone means
Only my own nightmares disturb me,
Few and far between,
When the disappointment of love gone wrong
Lingers only in my neighbor's bed.

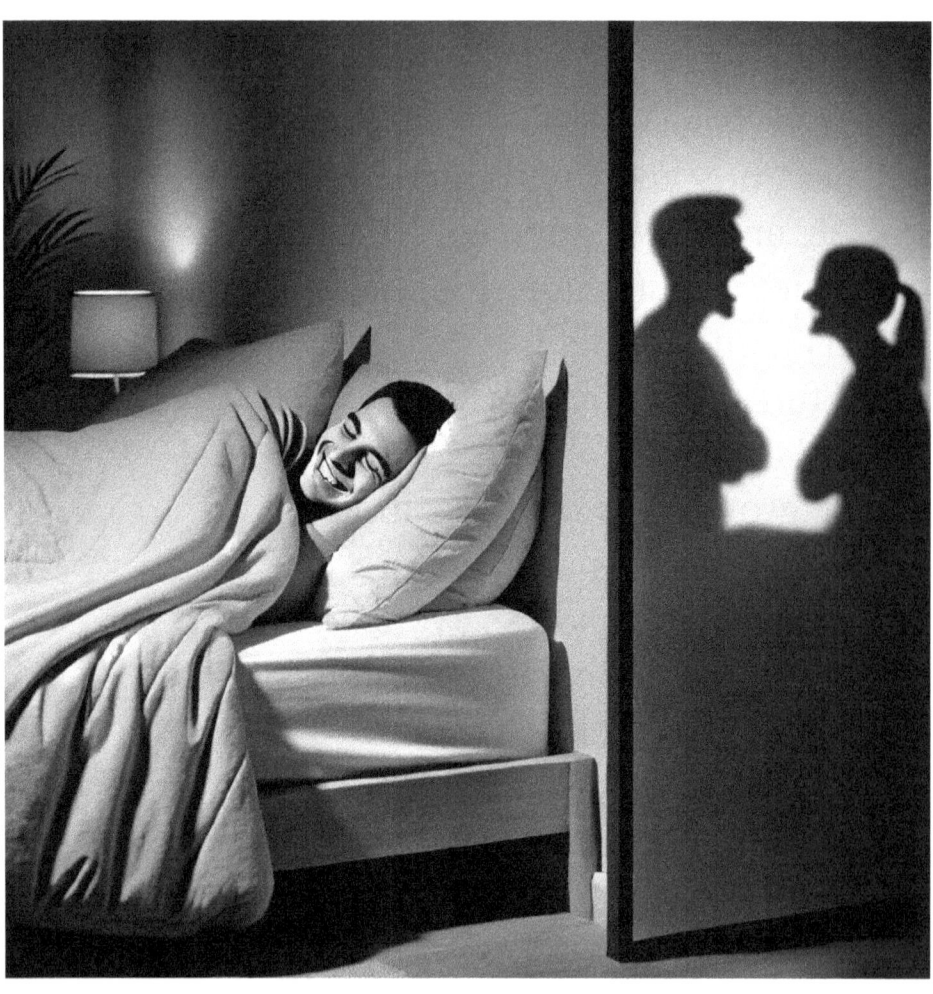

Me:

Chace me and I will run,
Flee and I will give chase,
for it is not in our nature for simple touch,
This game must be played
to satisfy our social interactions,
And I am over this thought I fear
I am over my desire to put up with you
I am over this useless cycle my dear
I am over the idea that I'm supposed to put up with you,
Sleeping alone means,
never waking because your partner rolled over,
sleep alone means,
I'm only affected by my nightmares,
which are few and far between,
when disappointment of love gone wrong,
roam only in my neighbors' bed,

ChatGPT:

Once more, I find myself on this road,
Mentally journeying to some unknown place.
My thought process remains within the norm,
And if such a place exists,
I intend to find it.

For again, I am here alone,
Struggling against the current,
Where keeping my head above water
Is a constant challenge.

Once more, I move as one,
The two I hoped to become
Never appearing on the horizon.
So the quest for another new sanctuary
Must be made alone.

Perhaps my mind is slipping,
Or maybe I have selective memories—
I don't recall these many mental struggles
Developing issues I never had before.
My life has become a roller coaster,
Fluctuating between extreme light and darkness
Every day,

And that can't be healthy.

Perhaps I am simply a runner,
Destined never to find peace while my shoes still tread.
Whatever the case,
It has become clear
This place isn't for me.

As I raise my sail once again
And let the breeze guide me,
I am reminded of another time,
Another place I have yet to explore.
It remains a memory,
Returning to my fantasies
Like an old friend coming home—

A time and place where I might find a kindred spirit,
A twin soul with a similar dream and prayer,
A hunger to be more than I am,
And to be loved for the imperfect dreamer that I am.

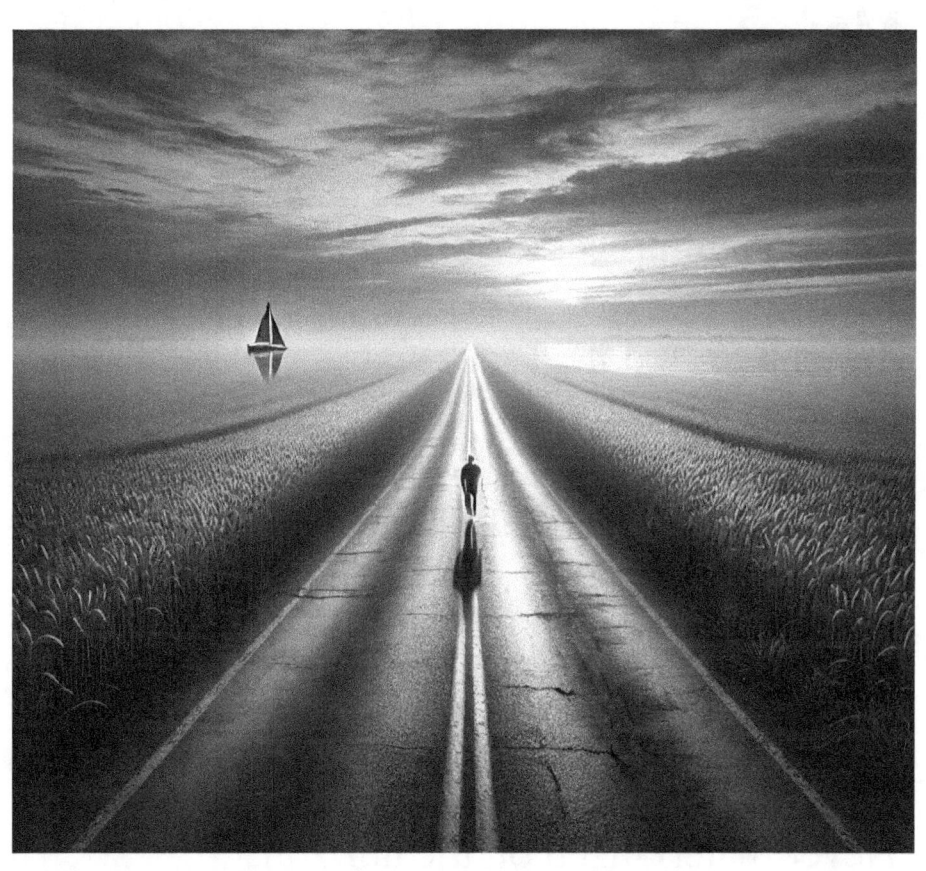

Me:

Again I find myself on this road,
Mentally traveling to somewhere
My thought process is of the norm
If that place exists
I intend to find it
Because once again,
I am here alone
Moving in the opposite direction of the current,
Where head above water is so difficult to maintain
Again
I move on as one,
The two I had hoped to become
Never materialized on the horizon,
So the journey to yet another new sanctuary
Must be made alone,
Perhaps my mind is slipping
Perhaps I have selective memories
I don't recall having this many mental problems,
Developing issues, I have never had before,
My life has become a roller coaster of manic
Extreme light and extreme darkness
Everyday,
And that can't be healthy

Perhaps I am simply a runner
Who will never find peace as long as my shoes have tread,
Whatever the case may be
It has become apparent
This isn't the place for me
And as I raise my sail yet again
And allow the breeze to blow me again
I am reminiscent of another time
Another place
That I have yet to explore
But is still a memory
Because it has returned to my fantasies
Like an old friend come home,
A time and place where I may find a kindred
A twin soul with a similar desire
A similar dream and prayer to the father
A hunger to be more than me
And loved for the imperfect dreamer that I am.

ChatGPT:

It sneaks up on me,
At unexpected moments,
No matter what I'm doing,
Everything stops,
Everything fades,
And all I see is her face,
Showing her pain,
Struggling to control it,

Because my face says "quit the nonsense,"
Her eyes plead for mercy,
And my cold heart,
Deep in denial,
Refused that mercy for a flawed theory—
"You need exercise,
You need to leave the house,
You're just depressed,
Get a job,
A sense of purpose might ease this pain."

All my life, I've wished for time travel,
To go back 20 years and share everything I know now.
That silent prayer has turned into an inner scream,

Begging my soul for another chance,
To redo those six months,
For I can't escape the image of her hospital bed,
Her silent voice still speaking,
When she pushed my hand away,
Realizing it wasn't my sister's.

I was asked to bear witness,
And no words came,
Though she asked for them—
A sonnet, an expression of my love,
An expression that never came,
And still hasn't come.

How do you describe such a relationship?
How do you explain the deep love and loathing?
She played many roles in this drama—
Mother, nemesis, friend,
Burden, support system, therapist,
Bully, and the reason I am who I am.

When it had to be done, I did it,
If I could convince someone else, I would,
I found humor in any situation—

Because she once mooned me during Freddie's nightmare.
She was my first real friend,
When my cousins said I wasn't friend material,
She was my first guidance counselor,
Offering advice I'm still grappling with.

She contributed to my self-esteem issues,
Because I never looked as she wished,
Didn't walk like the girl she wanted to raise,
Wouldn't wear a skirt,
Not even to her own funeral,
Where I sat in slacks,
Head held high,
Trying to channel her strength,
Trying to act as she did
At her mother's funeral—

She sat dry-eyed,
Head high,
Back stiff,
Storing her pain for private moments.
I too shut off my emotions that day,
Believing I made her proud,
Though with her, one could never be sure.

Perhaps she would have felt more connected

With me draped across her coffin,
Perhaps my wails of despair
Would have been music to her decomposing ears.
The world may never know.

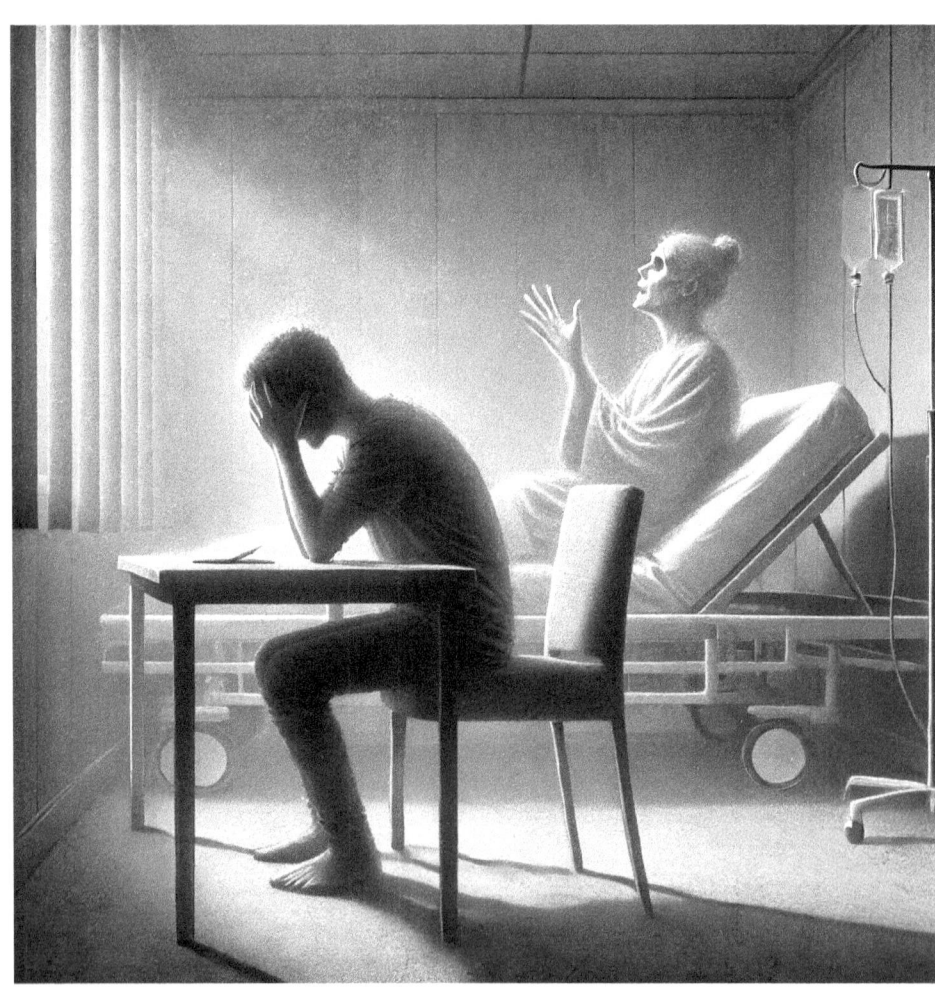

Me:

It just creeps up on me,
Some moments
No matter what I am doing,
All things stop,
Everything fades
And all I see is her face
Telling me she's in pain
Fighting to control that pain
Because my face is saying quit the bullshit,
Her eyes,
Pleading with me for mercy,
And my cold heart,
So deep in denial
Refused that mercy in exchange for a dead wrong theory,
You need exercise,
You need to leave the house
You're just depressed is all,
You need to get a job,
Perhaps a sense of purpose will diminish this pain,
My entire life,
I have been wishing for time travel,
I wanted to go back 20 years,
To tell me everything I know now,

Now that silent prayer has become and inner screaming
Begging with my very soul,
Give me another chance to do those 6 months over,
Cause I can't get past the image of her hospital bed,
Her inability to speak
Yet speaking still
When she pushes my hand away
Because she realized it was not my sisters,
And I am asked to bare witness,
And no words will come,
Because she asked for the words
More than once
In those final 6 months,
She asked me for a sonnet
An expression of my love,
An expression that never came to me,
Still hasn't come to me,
How do you describe that relationship?
How do you explain the deep love/loath?
She had more than one part in this play,
She was mother,
Nemeses
Friend,
Burden,

Support system,
Therapist,
Bully,
And reason why I am who I am,
When its gotta get done I do it,
When I can convince someone else I will,
I can find humor in any situation
Because my mother mooned me during
Freddie's nightmare,
She was my first real friend
When my cousins convinced me I wasn't friend material,
She was my first guidance counselor
Giving advice I am still recovering from,
She was a major contributor to my self-esteem issues,
Because I never looked the way she planned for me to look,
Because I didn't walk like the girl she wanted to raise,
Because she couldn't pay me to wear a skirt,
Not even to her own funeral,
Where I sat in slacks,
Head high,
Trying to channel her energy,
Trying to behave as if I were her,
13 years earlier at her own mother's funeral,

She sat with dry eyes,
Head high,
Back stiff as a board
Storing her pain for her private time,
I too refused access to my emotions that day,
I believed I made my mother proud,
But one can never tell with my mother,
Perhaps she would have been more in tuned with me draped across her coffin,
Perhaps my wails despair would have been music to her decomposing ears,
The world may never know.

ChatGPT:

It's not you that I desire,
It's the emotions you evoke,
The motivation you inspire.
I've never wanted anything
Quite like your spoiled princess demeanor.
My queen will crown me in return,
But what I really wanted
Was to behave as I did for you.
I once felt something similar
For a girl too young to appreciate the gifts I offered.
My longing to be more consumed me,
But when she left, so did that desire,
And the lethargic side of me returned,
Though not entirely.
I was a restless soul when we met,
With more energy than the unambitious should possess.
My indifferent façade fell away when you called my name.
But it's not you I want.
I want to grow for myself,
Just as I grew for you.

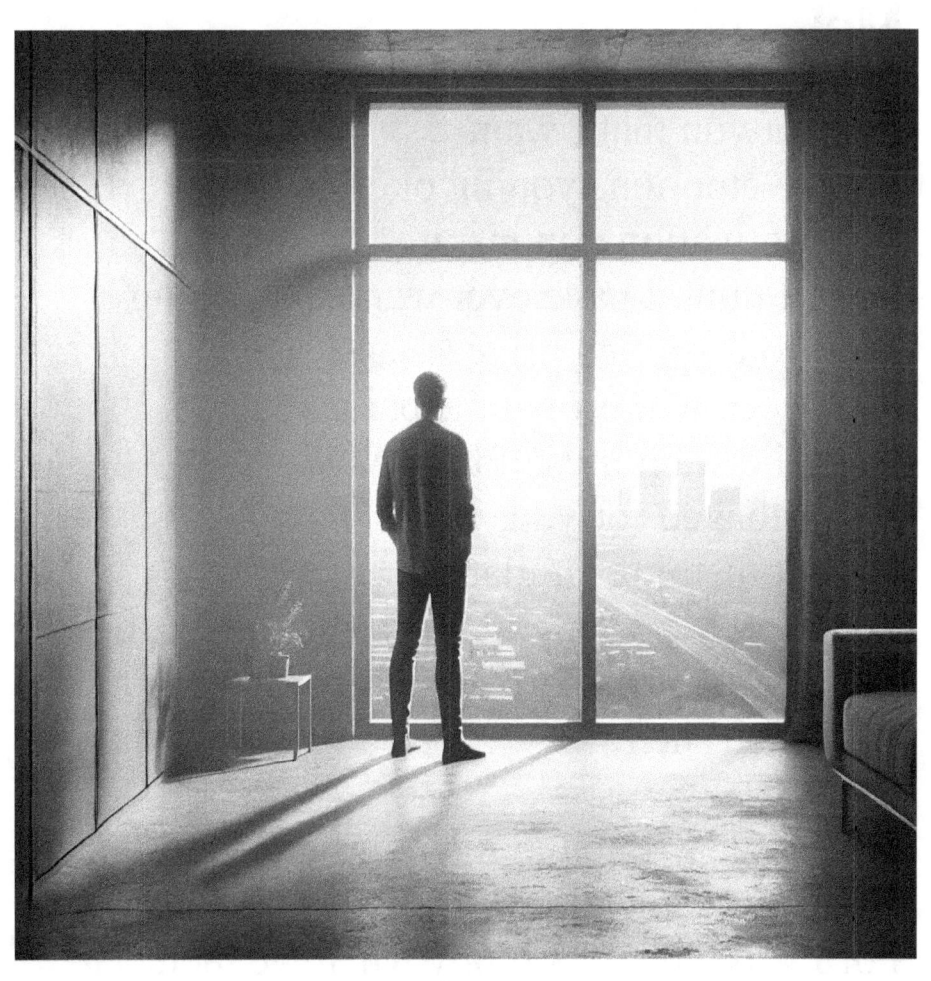

Me:

It is not you that I want,
It's the emotions you invoke,
The motivation you inspire,
I don't think I have ever wanted anything
Like your spoiled princess ass,
My queen will crown me back,
But I did want myself to behave
As I behaved for you,
I felt something similar once,
For a girl too young to know the gifts I offered,
My desire to be more was all consuming me,
But when she left,
It left,
And the lazy bitch in me returned,
But not completely,
For I was a restless hippy when we met,
With more energy than the unambitious should have,
My don't give a damn disguise fell away when you called my name,
But it's not you that I want,
I want to grow for me,
The way I grew for you.

ChatGPT:

When our eyes meet, and only I am moved,
I know I must steer clear of my desire.
I am a warrior without armor,
And each moment spent in her presence
Is another chance for the wound to deepen.
I am defenseless against her gaze,
Helpless against the sound of her voice.
Each brush of her skin is a hammer to my chest.
My thoughts spiral out of control
Whenever she is near.
I am placing myself in harm's way,
And when she speaks my name,
I remind myself:
I am not her choice.
She desires another.
So I will avoid her eyes,
I will scorn her smile,
I will convince myself she is a temptress,
Because to do anything else
Is to embrace defeat.

Me:

When eyes lock and only I am effected,
I think it's best that I steer clear of my desire,
For I am like a warrior with no body armor,
The more time I spend in the space of my adversary,
The more likely I am for injury,
For I am unable to protect myself from her eyes,
I am unable to shield myself from her voice,
And each brush of her skin is like blunt objects striking my chest,
I don't have the power to stop my thought process,
When she is near,
I am needlessly placing myself in harms way,
When she says my name,
I am unnecessarily reminding myself
That I am not her choice,
She would rather another,
So I will avoid her eyes,
I will detest her smile,
I will force myself to believe she be a minx,
Because to do anything else
Is setting myself up for failure

And in matters of my heart,
I prefer to win

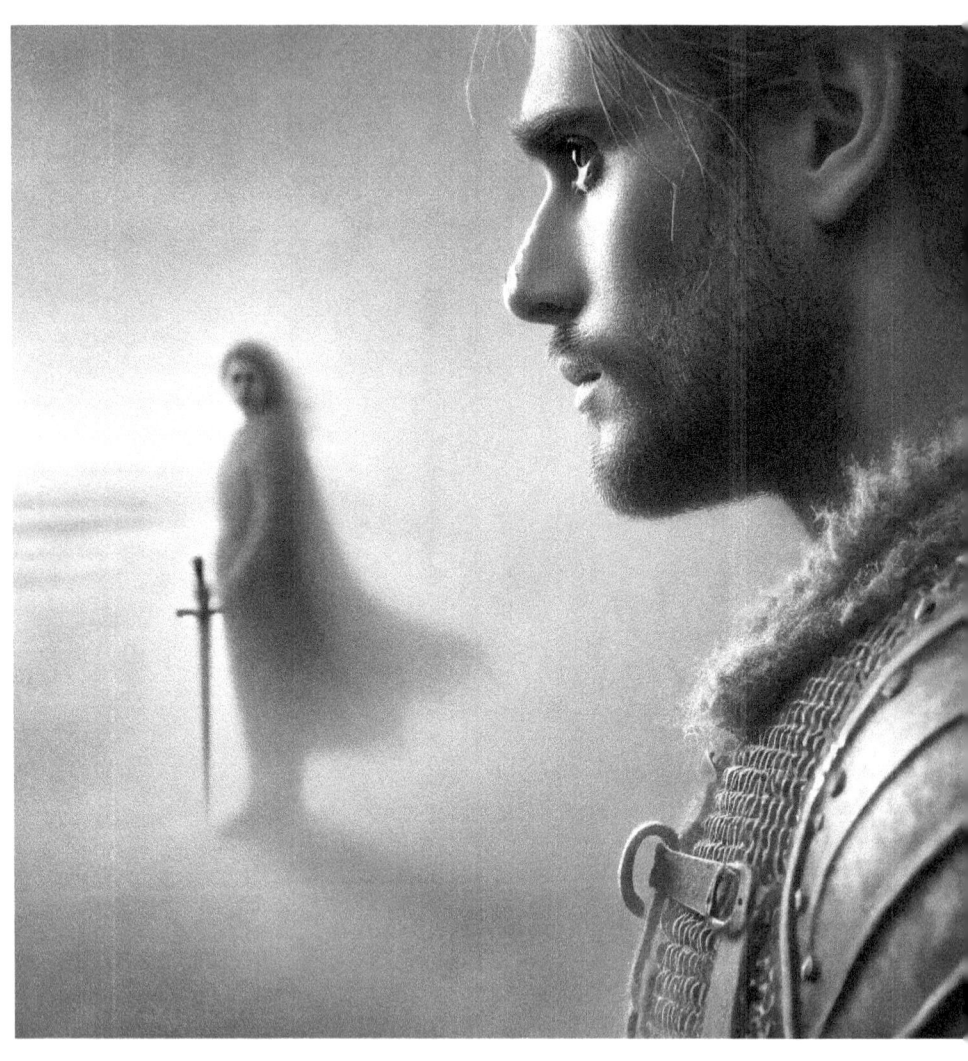

Me:

When eyes lock and only I am effected,
I think it's best that I steer clear of my desire,
For I am like a warrior with no body armor,
The more time I spend in the space of my adversary,
The more likely I am for injury,
For I am unable to protect myself from her eyes,
I am unable to shield myself from her voice,
And each brush of her skin is like blunt objects striking my chest,
I don't have the power to stop my thought process,
When she is near,
I am needlessly placing myself in harms way,
When she says my name,
I am unnecessarily reminding myself
That I am not her choice,
She would rather another,
So I will avoid her eyes,
I will detest her smile,
I will force myself to believe she be a minx,
Because to do anything else

Is setting myself up for failure
And in matters of my heart,
I prefer to win

ChatGPT:

And now, I pray for freedom—
For the strength to lift my head high,
And proclaim to the world:
I love what I do,
And mean it.
The lie won't save me;
I need it to be the truth.
I long to rise from my bed with ease,
To embrace the day with open arms,
To dance with my oatmeal.
I need to live my truth.
And I am ready for that truth,
For the daily grind of morning traffic,
If it leads to my happy place,
Where I am proud of my work,
And I work with pride,
With heart,
With passion.
Where my spirit is fully expressed,
And my time is running out.
The clock is ticking,
And soon I might get stuck,
Like my mother before me,
Like her mother before her.
We all passed before we were considered old,

But unlike them,
I will leave no one to mourn my smile,
No children to carry my name.
When I go, I will disappear,
Unless I leave a legacy in my work.
But that legacy cannot be born
While I despise what I do.
So, I pray for my dreams to leap from night to day,
To give birth to my legacy,
Before it's too late.

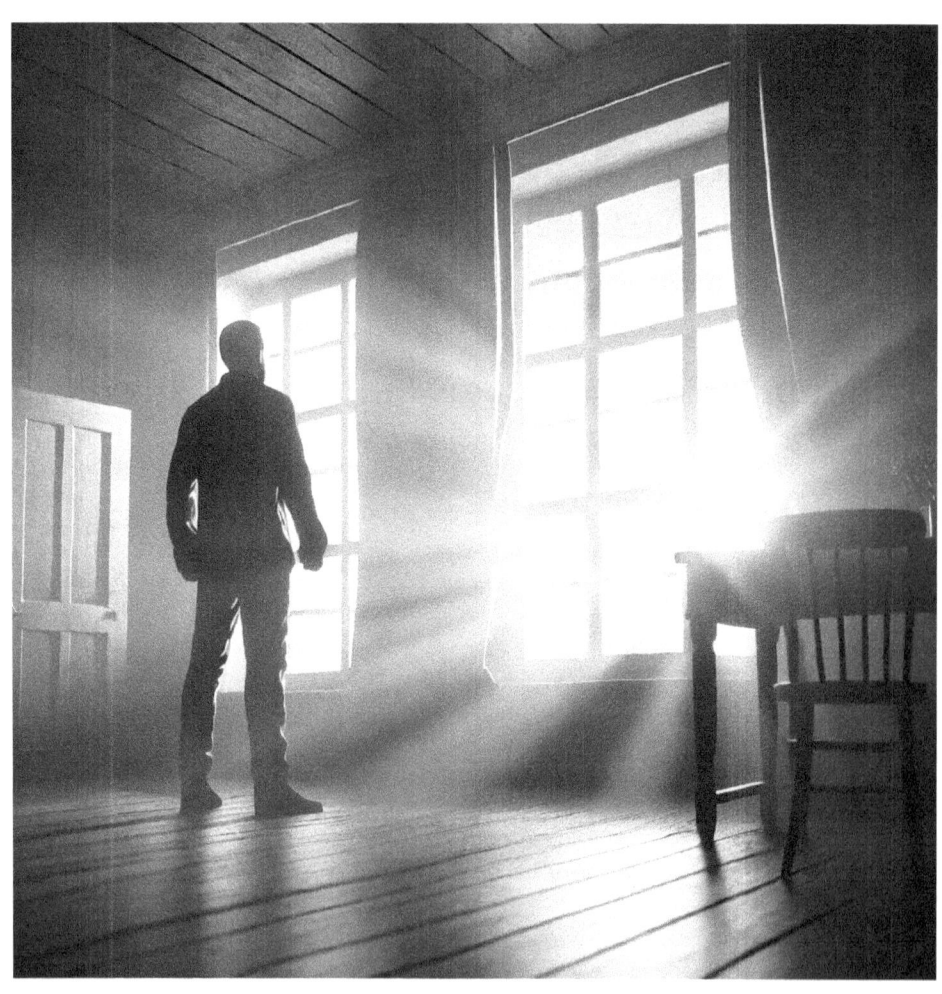

Me:

And now I pray for freedom,
For the ache to hold my head up,
And say to the masses,
I enjoy what I do,
And mean it,
Because the lie won't help my situation,
I need it to be the truth,
To need not force the spring from my bed,
To leap for my day,
To dance with my oatmeal,
I need to be living my truth,
And I am ready for that truth,
And the constant irritation of my morning traffic,
As long as that traffic is heading to my happy place,
Where I am proud of what I do,
And I do what I do proudly,
With heart,
And passion
And my personality being exploited,
And my time is running out,
This clock is ticking,
Not long before I get stuck,
Where my mother got stuck,

And her mother got stuck,
And we all die before we are considered old,
And unlike them,
I will have no mourners to miss my smile,
No offspring to carry my genes,
I will cease when I go,
Unless I leave a legacy with my work,
Which isn't going to happen,
While I hate what I do,
So I pray that my dreams jump from my night,
And into my day,
And I can give birth to my legacy,

ChatGPT:

Our first meeting was all wrong,
Yet it lingers in my mind,
A memory that won't let go.
I was tangled in a relationship,
One I should have left behind.
You weren't there for me—
But you should have been.
There was a spark between us,
Undeniable, electric,
The moment our eyes met.
But timing was our enemy,
And what could have been
Remains a distant possibility.
I wish it were different.
I wish we had met under better circumstances,
Where all we knew were our first names,
And the pull of attraction in those first few moments.
I regret burying my feelings,
And I yearn to quiet this silent wish.
I wish there were a chance for us,
Instead of being caught in this endless loop,
A cycle you never cared for,
A taste I wish I hadn't developed.
If I could turn back time,

If today I had the courage,
I'd close one door and open yours.
I'd pursue you, no pretense, no games.
In your arms, I'd find my peace,
And you would find your home in mine.
If only things were different,
If time travel were real,
There would be a place for you and me.

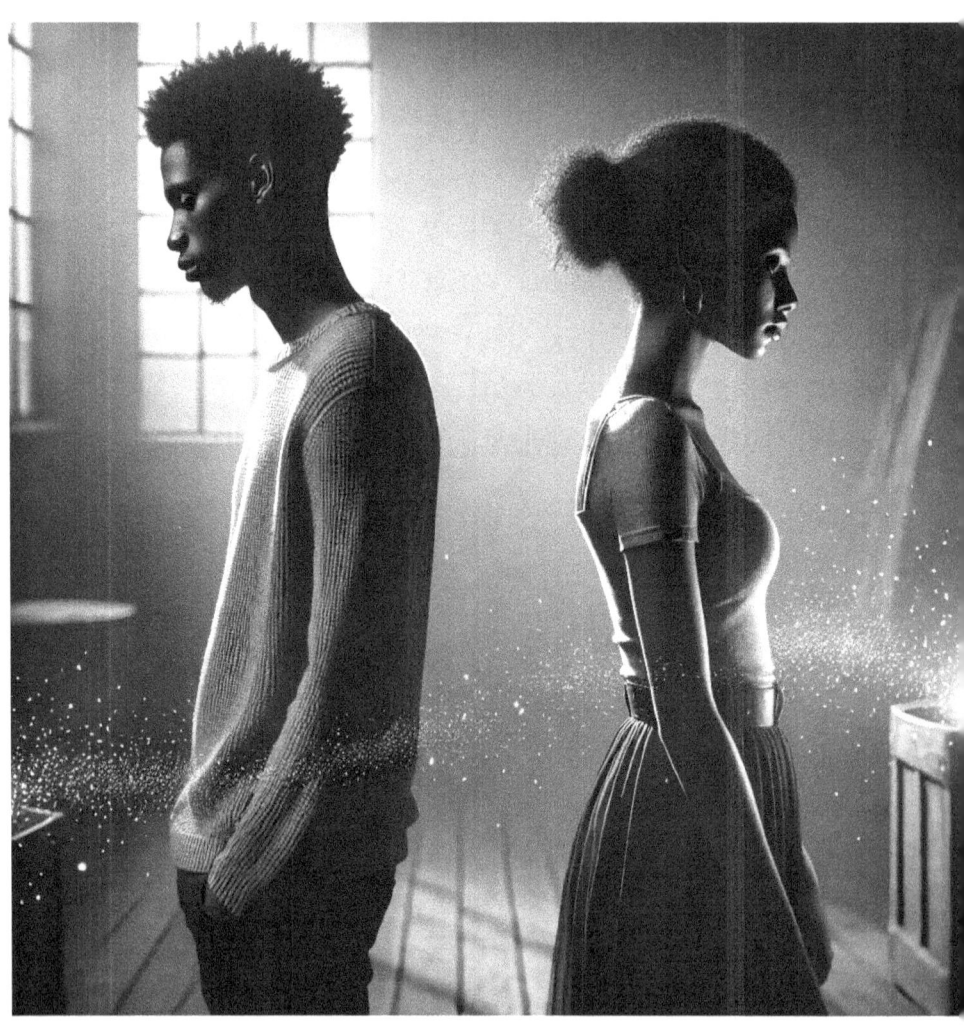

Me:

Our first meeting was all wrong.
But for the sake of this crush
It still sticks in my head
I was in a relationship
I should have gotten out
You were not there to see me,
You should have been,
There was a spark between us,
I felt it the first time our eyes met,
Timing was our enemy,
It didn't happen then
And it may never happen now,
I wish it were otherwise.
I wish we had met under other circumstances.
I wish the only information we knew about
each other was our first names and the mutual
attraction we shared those first few meetings.
I wish I hadn't ignored my feelings
I wish I could stop making this silent wish.
I wish there was a chance for us
Instead of the inner crossings of this crazy
circle that you never had a taste for,
I wish I had never developed a taste for it.

If I could go back in time,
I wish that now, today, I had a spine,
I swear
I'd close a door and open yours.
I'd pursue you and say fuck a bullshit friendship.
I'd be happy in your arms and you would find your home in mine.
If things were different,
If time travel was possible,
There would be a place for you and me.

Our first encounter was all wrong,
But in the realm of this infatuation,
It remains etched in my mind.
I was entangled in a relationship's web,
One I should have severed long ago.
You weren't there to witness it,
But you should have been,
For there was an undeniable spark between us,
One I felt the instant our gazes intertwined.
Yet, timing conspired against us,
Preventing our connection from blossoming then,
And perhaps, it may never come to fruition now.
I wish circumstances were different,

That our knowledge of each other was limited to our first names,
And the mutual attraction that pulsed between us during those initial encounters.
I regret suppressing my feelings,
And I yearn to silence this silent wish.
I wish there was a glimmer of hope for us,
Instead of us being trapped in the confines of this endless loop,
A cycle you never cared to entertain.
I wish I had never acquired a taste for it.
If time could be rewound,
If only today I possessed the courage,
I'd shut one door and open yours,
I'd pursue you unabashedly, forsaking the facade of mere friendship.
In your embrace, I'd find solace,
And you'd discover your sanctuary within mine.
If circumstances were different,
If time travel were within reach,
There would exist a place where you and I could exist together

ChatGPT:

Did you just ask why I'm so arrogant?
Well, aren't you the good little Christian,
All judgmental and sanctified.
Yesterday, you laughed with me,
Shared your bread, called me friend.
But today, you found we don't share the same faith—
Now I'm unworthy of your smile,
Unworthy of your table,
Not even fit to be called dog, let alone friend.

How wonderful your faith must be,
Or is it your church?
Whichever one is teaching this hate.
How holy your priest must feel,
Casting stones without fear,
As the translations of your book grow funnier each year.

You celebrate what you once condemned—
Do you even know how many pagan rituals you practice?
Atoning for sins that were never yours to claim.

Who are you to say what my soul has traveled
here for?
Who are you to lead me?
Shepherds need not apply;
I hear my Father's voice within my heart.

I know the difference between right and
wrong.
Why is it okay for you to follow a man in a
robe,
But blasphemous for me to follow my own
heart?
Isn't it enough that I do unto others,
That I turn the other cheek?
Why must I kneel at your altar?

Have you not noticed your Sabbath
Is starting to resemble a rock concert?
Your humble walls are anything but humble.
Haven't you noticed?
Yours is the richest nation there is.
I remember your teachings—
It's easier for a camel to pass through the eye
of a needle—
But still, you pass your collection plate long
past what's needed to sustain you.

And you call me arrogant.
Even though I believe that money is the root,
That greed is the enemy—
It's why I avoid you.
And you say I'm arrogant?
Because I'm proud of my education,
My smile,
My ability to survive everything life has thrown at me,
Including you.
Especially you.

It's you that has made this so damn hard.
I'm arrogant because I believe I've found my truth,
That I don't need you,
Just this smile I'm wearing
And the people who love me.
I'm arrogant because I don't fear my Father's sword,
Because while you cower with your head bowed,
I stand bravely before Him,
With my knowing heart.

And I openly admit,
I do not know your answers, Father,

It's not for me to ask those questions.
But I'm grateful for my pulse, Father,
And I'll cherish it until my dying breath.

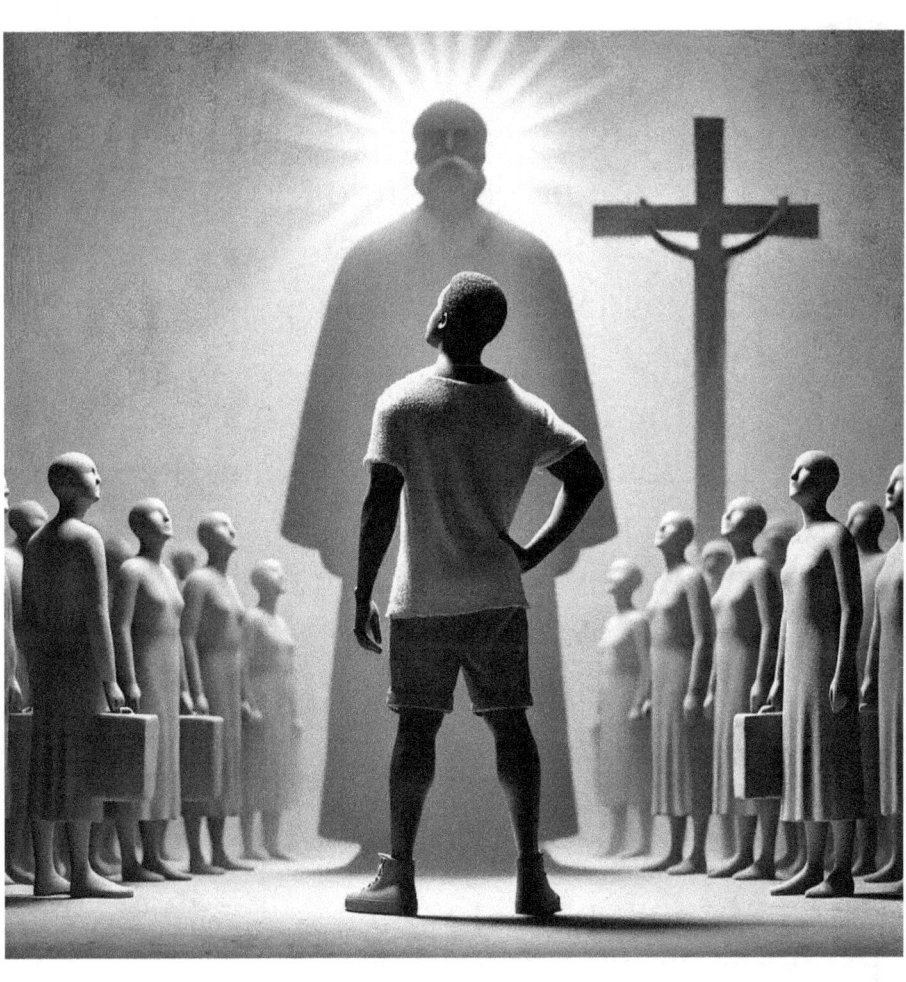

Me:

Did you just ask me why I'm so arrogant?
Well aren't you the good little Christian?
All judgmental like,
Yesterday you laughed with me,
Ate with me,
Called me friend,
And today you found we don't share the same faith,
So now I'm not worthy of your smile
I'm not worthy of your bread,
Not someone you'd call dog let alone friend,
How wonderful your faith
Or you're church
Which ever one is teaching this hate,
How holy your priest must be
Throwing stones without fear,
The translations of your book get funnier with each passing year,
The celebrations for things once condemned
Do you know how many pagan rituals you practice?
The atonement for what has never been your right,
Who are you to say what my soul has traveled here for?

Who are you to lead me?
Shepard's need not apply,
For I can hear my fathers wishes within this heart of mine.
I can easily detect the difference between right and wrong,
Why is it ok for you to follow a man in a skirt?
And blasphemous for me to follow my own heart?
Isn't it enough that I do on to others?
Isn't it enough that I turn the other cheek?
Why must I bow and sweep at your alter?
Have you not noticed your Sabbath is starting to resemble a rock concert?
That your humble walls are anything but humble?
Haven't you noticed?
Yours is the richest nation there is,
And as I was once like you,
I remember your teachings
It's easier for a camel to enter the eye of a needle
But still you past your collection plates long past what is needed to sustain you,
And you call me arrogant,
Even thou I truly believe that money be the root,

That greed be the enemy,
And it is thus which makes me avoid you,
And you say I am arrogant?
Because I'm proud of my education
And my smile,
And my ability to survive everything this life has thrown at me,
Including you,
Especially you,
It's you that has made this so damn hard,
I'm arrogant because I believe I have found my truth,
That I don't need you
Just this smile that I'm wearing
And these people that love me
I'm arrogant because I can never fear my father's sword,
Because as you coward from him with your head bowed,
I stand bravely before him with my knowing heart.
And I openly admit,
I do not know your answers father,
It's not for me to ask those questions.
I am grateful for my pulse father
And I will enjoy it until my dying breath.

ChatGPT:

Much like my own,
Your tongue spawns wonder,
With every word you breathe,
My heart mimic's thunder.
Mayhap a fool's paradise—
For a fool I would be,
If our stars aligned,
If the moon blessed thee.
I'd share with you my dreams,
Oh, the risks that I see,
In daring to make a dream real—
That you belong with me.

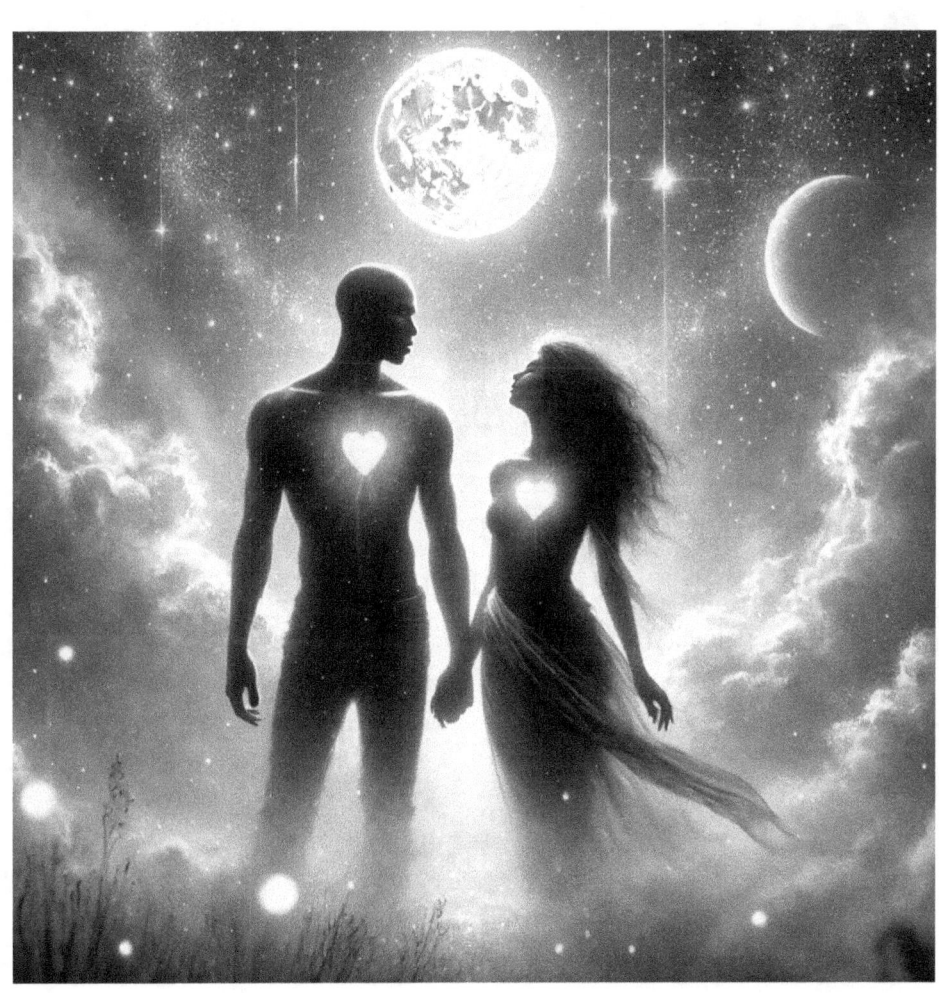

Me:

Much like mine own,
Your tongue spawns wonder,
with every word you breath,
My heart makes mimic of thunder,
Mayhap fool's paradise,
Cause your fool I would be,
if our stars aligned,
if the moon blessed thee,
I would share with you my dreams,
oh the risk that I see,
With trying to make dream happen,
of you belong with me,

ChatGPT:

If you didn't need your Beemer
And a perfect view of the setting sun,
If you could sleep without your castle,
I'd still not be the one.

If you could live without your diamonds,
If carats were just part of a meal,
If stocks and bonds, and Swiss accounts
Were not the things that made you feel—

If certainty lined my spine with substance,
And I could generate self-control like a pheromone,
If ambition fueled my every action,
I'd still find myself sleeping alone.

I'd still not be the woman to hold you,
I could never be your Jane.
I wouldn't dare to keep your fascination,
For I savor the taste of my pain.

So you, the mighty huntress,
With bigger fish to fry—
And me, the lowly poet,
I'm just lucky you let me try.

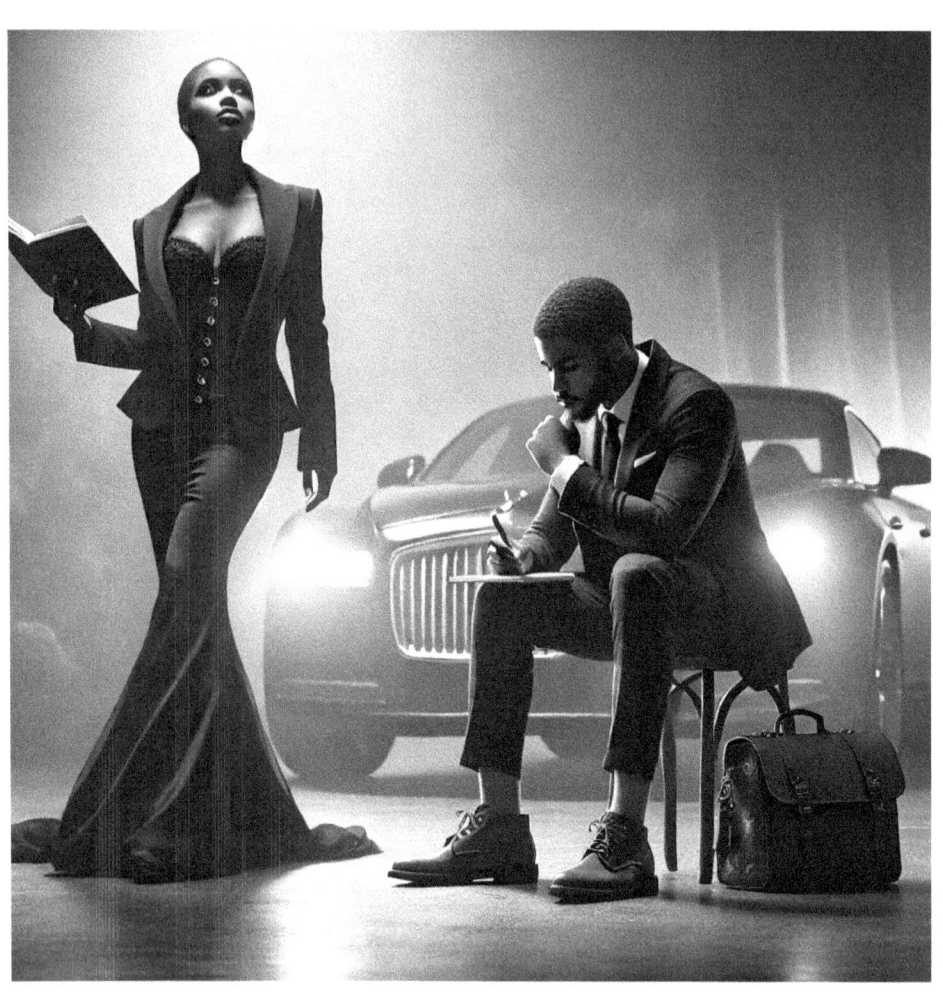

Me:

If you didn't need your Beemer
 And a perfect view of the setting sun,
If you could sleep without your castle,
I would still not be the one,
If you could live without your diamonds
If carrots were no more than your meal,
If stocks and bonds, and Swiss accounts,
 Were not the things that made you feel
If certainty lined my spine with substance,
And I could generate self control like a pheromone,
If ambition consumed my character,
I would still find myself sleeping alone,
I would still not be the woman who could hold you,
I could never be your Jane,
I couldn't think of retaining your fascination,
Because I enjoy retaining my pain,
So you the mighty huntress,
You got bigger fish to fry,
And me the lowly poet
I'm just lucky you let me try.

ChatGPT:

Sick of being dark and cold,
I long to stand in the light,
To absorb the energy I need
To keep fighting this fight.

I've let myself be wrapped in shadows,
Negativity's grip too tight,
Starving myself of vital warmth,
Just to pay bills and survive the night.

I know where my happiness lies,
But I've lingered in exile too long,
I must remind myself each day
That the shade is where I don't belong.

Though darkness may flatter my form,
To stand in the sun is my right,
For I'm no creature of the night—
I am a child of the light.
Smiling in the sun, that's me,
Basking in warmth, wild and free.

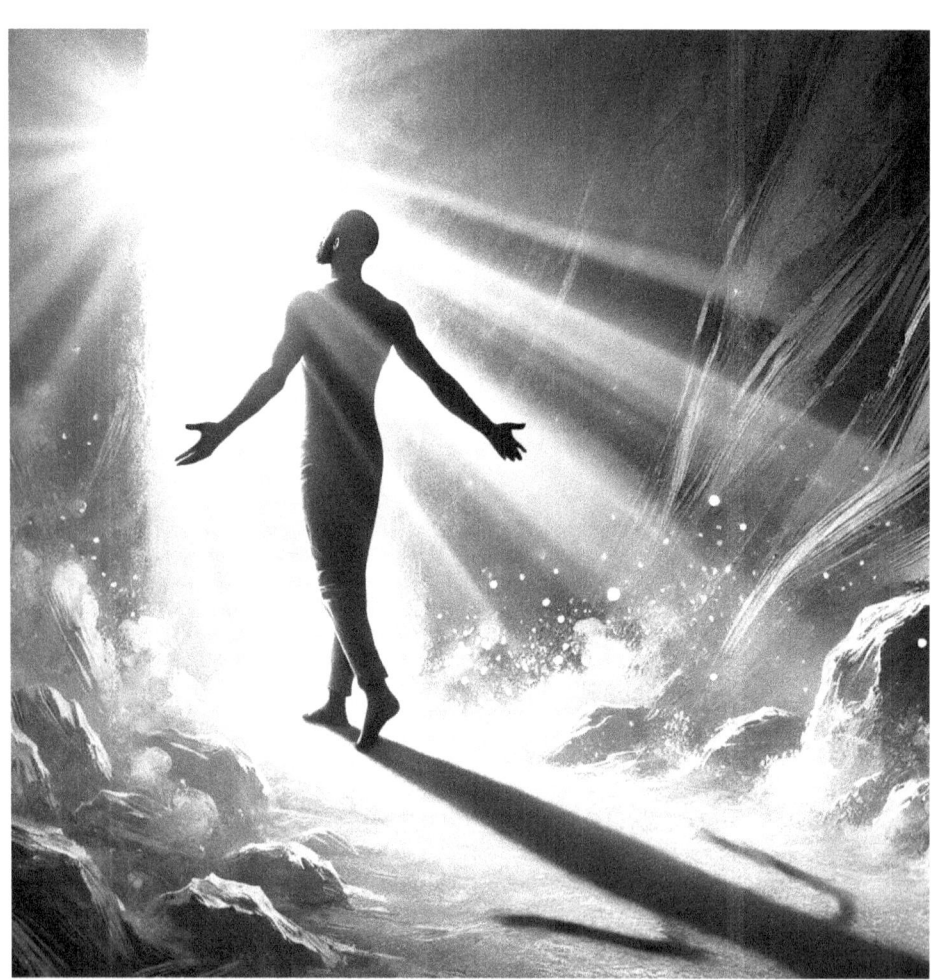

Me:

Sick of being dark and cold,
I want to stand in the light
Where I can absorbed the energy I need
To keep fighting this fight,

I've allowed myself to be surrounded by negative
When the positive is how I feed,
Starving myself of essential nutrients,
To pay bills, coexist and not lead,

I know how to find my happy place
And I've allowed my exile too long,
I need only to remind myself more often,
That the shade for me is wrong,

Although the dark looks good on me,
to stand in the sun is my free,
For I am no creature of the night,
I am a child of the light,
Smiling in the light is more me.

ChatGPT:

I wish I could allow myself
The joy you project
Each time you pass through my space,
But fear grips my spine,
Reminding me of the obvious.

I wish I could allow myself
The smile that sneaks across my face
Each time I realize, yes—
You're mocking me…
But self-esteem holds me back,
Convinced I'm nothing more
Than your weekend escape.

I wish we had met
Under circumstances
That allowed us to explore
Every emotion, completely.
Yet I'm grateful to know
That feeling still lives in me,
That a beautiful smile
And inviting eyes
Have jump-started my heart,
Returning me to myself.

I wish I could read your mind,
To understand the nature of your smile.
I've been fooled before,
Or perhaps I've read too much into a glance.
I wish to see how far this could go,
But fear whispers that we've run our course.

I wish, for once in my life,
To abandon all wishes, assumptions, fears, and faults,
And simply savor the feeling you've stirred in me.
And I pray I've stirred the same in you.
But fear—damn fear—
And foolish pride,
And my need to hide,
As always, take command of this journey.

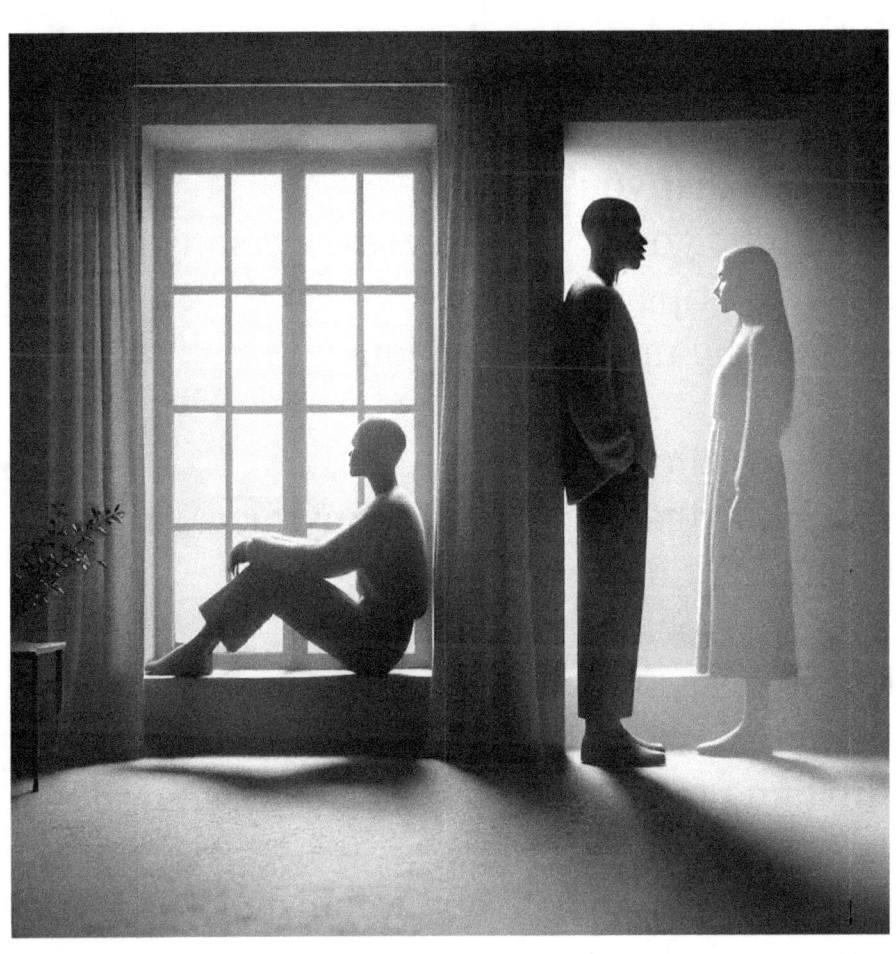

Me:

I wish to allow myself
This joy that you project
Each time you travel threw my personal space,
But fear grips my spine
Reminding me of the obvious,

I wish to allow myself
The smile that creeps across my face
Each time I realize that yes…
You are mocking me..
But self esteem issues prevent me
From believing I would be
Anything more than your weekend getaway,

I wish we had met under circumstances
That would have allowed
For complete explorations of all emotions,
But I am grateful for the knowledge
That feeling in me has not died,
And a beautiful smile
And inviting eyes
Has jump started my reality again,
I feel like I have returned to my body,

I wish that I could read your mind

So that I may know the nature of your smile,
I have been easily fooled in the past,
Or simply read to much into a smile,
I wish to see how far this could go
But my fear is we have run our course,

I wish for once in my life
To forgo all wishes, assumptions, fears and faults,
And simply enjoy the feeling you evoked in me
And I pray I project the same in you.
But fear, damn fear,
And foolish pride,
And my need to hide
As usual take command of this journey.

ChatGPT:

I can't sell my soul—
It doesn't belong to me.
It belongs to my creator,
And I've come to believe
My creator will want it back when I'm done.
It can't have any chips or cracks,
Because I won't get my deposit back.

I can't sell my integrity—
It belongs to my peace of mind.
I treasure sleep far too much
To trade it for folding paper.
Sure, the paper's nice,
Useful, even,
But it's not worth more than a night of dreams.

I can sell my work,
But only the pieces that don't cling to my heart.
My imagination is a gift,
But my heart is a blessing.
And you can't charge someone for blessings,
For being true to yourself—
That's the one thing that must always remain free.

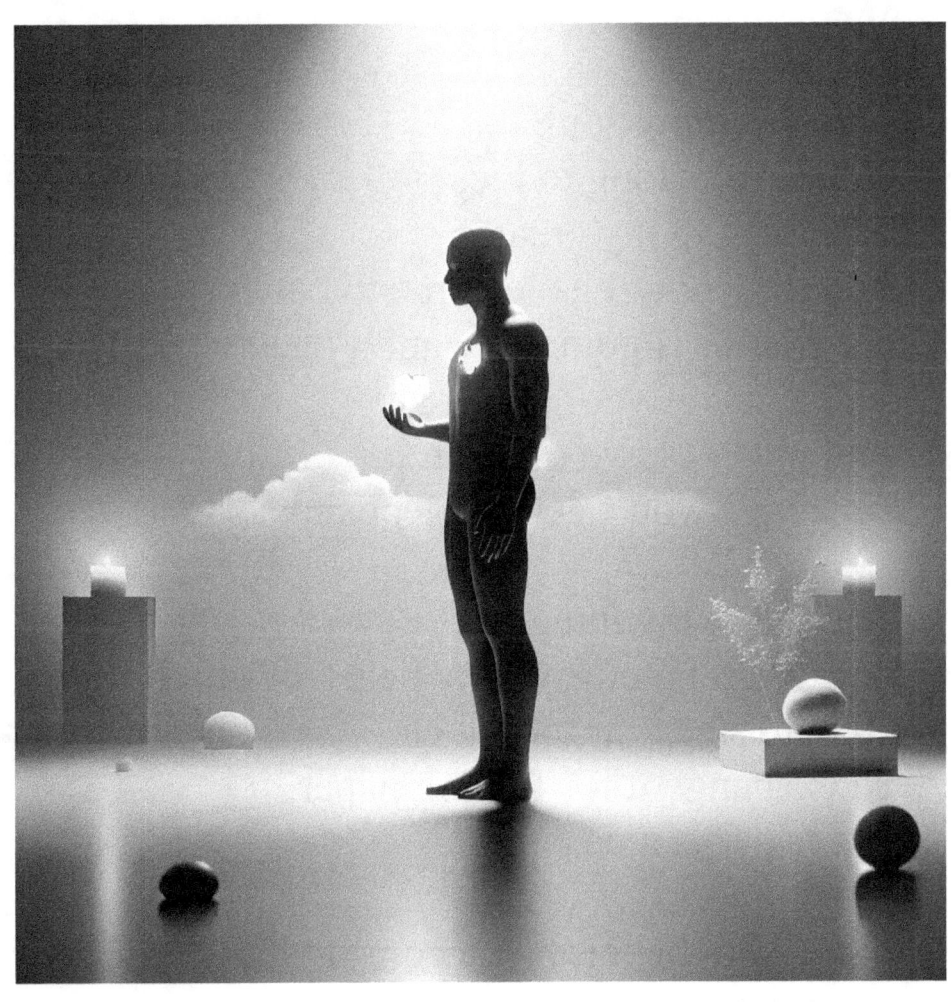

Me:

I can't sell my soul,
It doesn't belong to me,
It belongs to my creator,
And somehow I have come to believe,
My creator is going to want it back when I'm done,
And it can't have chips in it,
Because I won't get my deposit back,

I can't sell my integrity,
Because it belongs to my peace of mind,
I like to sleep far too much,
To exchange it for folding paper,
The paper is nice,
I find it useful,
But it's not better than a comfortable night of adventure

I can sell my work,
But only the things that aren't that close to my heart,
My imagination is a gift,
But my heart is a blessing
And I can't make someone pay for blessings
To be who I say I am,

Which is all I've ever wanted to be,
That stuff has to be free

ChatGPT:

I heard my voice, as the sun set on another adventure,
Realized it was this sound, this very echo,
Holding me back. My own singing,
Drowning out success, when silence
Could have won the day.

But I chose to scream instead.
Now I know—brilliance isn't self-proclaimed,
And being gifted doesn't cure poverty.
It's the recognition of strengths and weaknesses
That fills your belly, that softens your bed.

Embrace yourself, without demanding
Others do the same, and maybe they will.

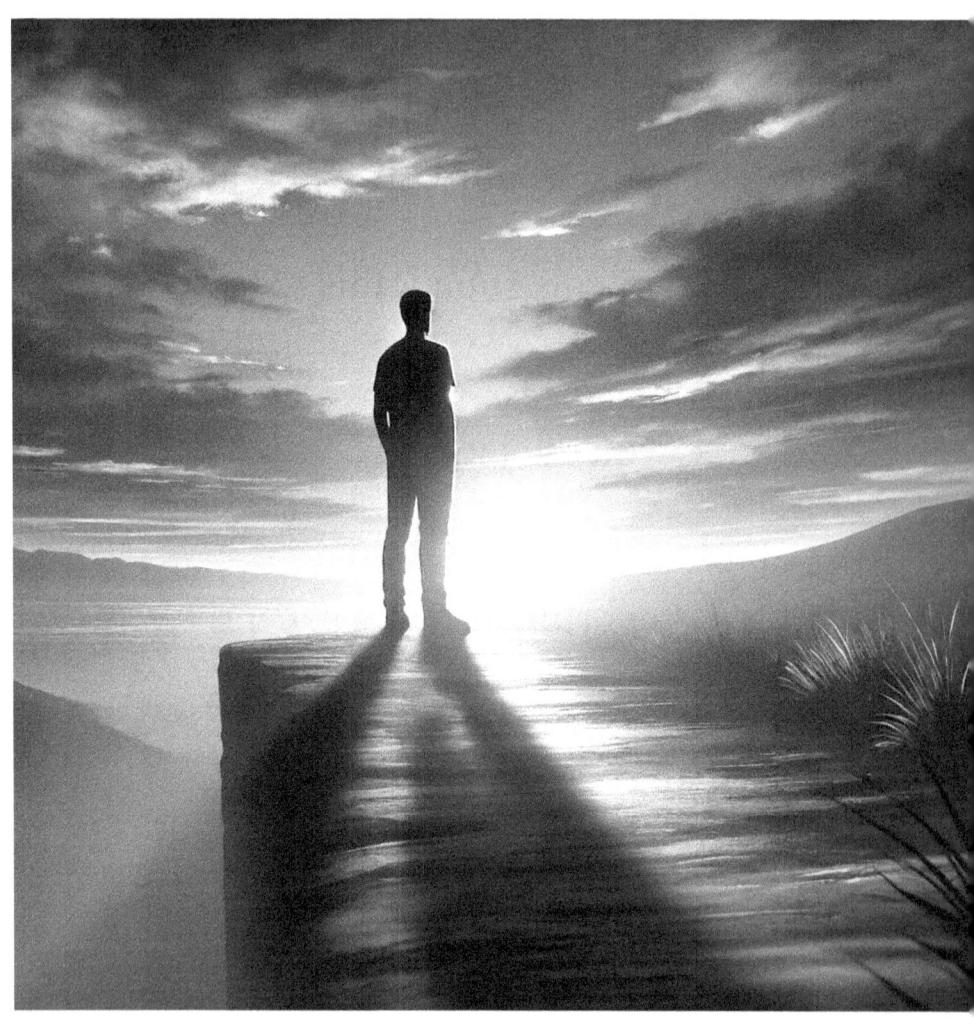

Me:

I heard my own voice,
 as the sun set on yet another adventure,
and realized it was this sound itself holding me back,
mine own singing,
 blocking out success,
 when silence would have won the day,
 I choose instead to scream,
 and Now I know,
 brilliance isn't self-proclaimed,
 gifted isn't the cure for poverty,
it's the realization of your strengths and weakness that will fill your belly,
 and crease your bed,
 embrace yourself,
without forcing others to embrace you too,
 and maybe they will.

www.ingramcontent.com/pod-product-compliance
Lightning Source LLC
Chambersburg PA
CBHW070143230526
45471CB00002B/498